D1526707

Our Animal World

Who Lays Eggs?

by Karen Latchana Kenney

1

Say hello to amicus readers.

You'll find our helpful dog, Amicus, chasing a ball—to let you know the reading level of a book.

Learn to Read

Frequent repetition of sentence structures, high frequency words, and familiar topics provide ample support for brand new readers. Approximately 100 words.

Read Independently

Repetition is mixed with varied sentence structures and 6 to 8 content words per book are introduced with photo label and picture glossary supports. Approximately 150 words.

Read to Know More

These books feature a higher text load with additional nonfiction features such as more photos, time lines, and text divided into sections. Approximately 250 words.

Amicus Readers are published by **Amicus**
P.O. Box 1329, Mankato, Minnesota 56002

Series Editor   Rebecca Glaser
Book Editor   Wendy Dieker
Series Designer   Kia Adams
Book Designer   Heather Dreisbach
Photo Researcher   Heather Dreisbach

Printed in the United States of America at Corporate Graphics in North Mankato, Minnesota.

1022
3-2011

10 9 8 7 6 5 4 3 2 1

Library of Congress Cataloging-in-Publication Data

Kenney, Karen Latchana.
   Who lays eggs? / by Karen Latchana Kenney.
      p. cm. – (Amicus readers. Our Animal World)
   Includes index.
   Summary: "A Level 1 Amicus Reader that describes different animals that lay eggs, describes the eggs, and explains where they are laid. Includes comprehension activity"–Provided by publisher.
   ISBN 978-1-60753-146-3 (library binding)
   1. Eggs–Juvenile literature. 2. Animals–Juvenile literature. I. Title.
   SF490.3.K46 2011
   591.4'68-dc22

                                              2010033481

Table of Contents

Pretty blue eggs sit in a robin's nest in a tree. Other animals lay eggs too. They all find ways to keep their eggs safe.

clutch

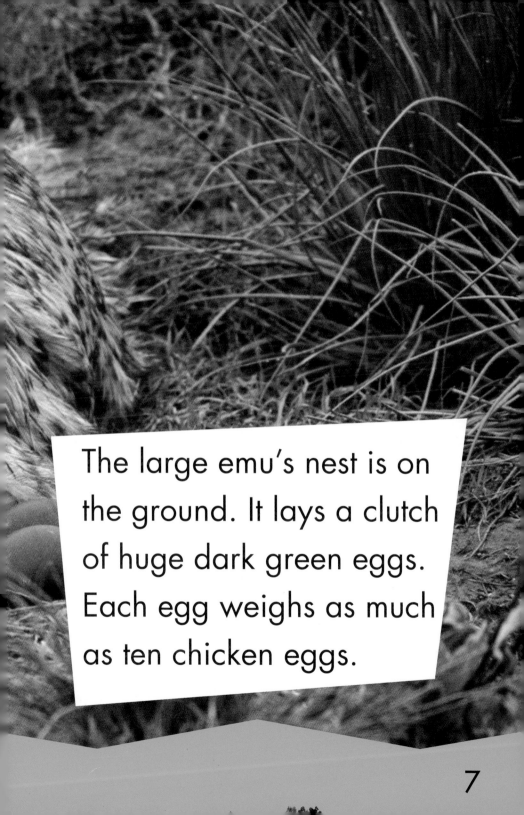

The large emu's nest is on the ground. It lays a clutch of huge dark green eggs. Each egg weighs as much as ten chicken eggs.

burrow

8

Like a duck, the platypus has a bill. It is not a bird, but it does lay eggs. In its burrow, the platypus lays one or two tiny eggs.

Crocodiles make nests in sand or dirt. When the babies hatch, they use a tiny egg tooth. It helps cut their shells open.

sac

Wolf spiders make silk
sacs for their eggs. The
mother carries the sac
on her body until the
eggs hatch.

A salamander lays its eggs in the water. A thick gel covers the eggs. It keeps other animals from eating them.

gel

In the ocean, squids
lay eggs in cases.
Many eggs are inside
each one.

A sea turtle lays her eggs on the sandy beach. Inside eggs, all kinds of animals grow. What would happen to them without their eggs?

Picture Glossary

burrow
a tunnel or hole in the ground that is made by an animal

case
a container for something that is held inside

clutch
a group of eggs laid around the same time

gel
a thick matter that
is like jelly

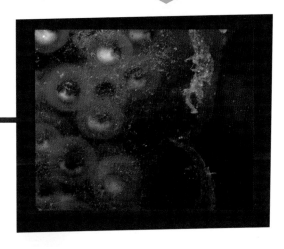

sac
something that is
shaped like a bag
or a pouch

shell
a hard covering
of an egg

21

What Do You Remember?

1. Trace this chart on a piece of paper.
2. For each animal, check the box that tells where each animal lays its eggs.

Animal	Nest	Burrow	Sac	Water
salamander				
emu				
wolf spider				
robin				
squid				
platypus				
crocodile				

If you don't remember, look back at the words and pictures in the book for the answers.

Ideas for Parents and Teachers

Our Animal World, an Amicus Readers Level 1 series, gives children fascinating facts about animals with lots of reading support. In each book, photo labels and a picture glossary reinforce new vocabulary. The What Do You Remember? activity page reinforces comprehension. Use the ideas listed below to help children get even more out of their reading experience.

Before Reading

- Look at the cover of the book. Discuss what it reveals about the book.
- Ask students: *What is an egg?* Then discuss the kinds of animals they know that lay eggs.
- Take a picture walk through the book. Ask students to discuss what they think they will learn about eggs.

During Reading

- Read the book aloud to students or have them read independently.
- Ask students to write an interesting fact they learned from each spread.
- Point out the glossary words in the text. Ask students to guess their definitions.

After Reading

- Look at the picture glossary. Have students check their definitions with the actual definitions.
- Use the What Do You Remember? activity on page 22 to help review the text.
- Discuss the different kinds of animals that lay eggs. Ask: *Which animals were you surprised to find out laid eggs?*

23

Index

Web Sites

Jean-Michel Cousteau's Ocean Futures Society: Market Squid
http://www.oceanfutures.org/learning/kids-cove/
creature-feature/market-squid

National Geographic Kids: Platypus
http://kids.nationalgeographic.com/Animals/CreatureFeature/
Platypus

Ohio State Parks: The Slinky Wolf Spider
http://www.dnr.state.oh.us/kidsthings/oct05/tabid/555/
Default.aspx

Photo Credits
Arco Images GmbH/Alamy, cover, 1; Bill Bachman/Alamy, 6–7, 20; Dave Watts/Alamy, 8, 20; DD Photography/Shutterstock, 4, 21; Fred Bavendam/Getty Images, 18; George Grall/Getty Images, 14–15, 21; Mark MacEwen/Photolibrary, 10; Tomas1111/Dreamstime.com, 12, 21; WaterFrame/Alamy, 16–17, 20

24